Lessons from the School of Healing

First Fruits Press
The Academic Open Press of Asbury Theological Seminary
204 N. Lexington Ave., Wilmore, KY 40390
859-858-2236
first.fruits@asburyseminary.edu
asbury.to/firstfruits

Lessons from the School of Healing

A series of articles originally published in The Herald from January 8th through June 11th 1975

by

Frank Bateman Stanger

First Fruits Press
Wilmore, Ky
c2015

Lessons from the School of Healing: A series of articles originally published in The Herald from January 8th through June 11th 1975 by Frank Bateman Stange

Published by First Fruits Press, © 2015
Digital version at
http://place.asburyseminary.edu/firstfruitsheritagematerial/86/

ISBN: 9781621711636 (print),
9781621711643 (digital), 9781621711650 (kindle)

Stanger, Frank Bateman.
    Lessons from the school of healing: a series of articles originally published in the Herald from January 8th through June 11th 1975 / by Frank Bateman Stanger.
    i, 102 p. ; 21 cm.
    Wilmore, Ky. : First Fruits Press, ©2015.
    This series appeared in the Herald, January 8-June 11, 1975
    Previously published: Wilmore, Kentucky : Asbury Theological Seminary, 1975.
    ISBN: 9781621711636 (pbk.)
    1. Spiritual healing. I. Title. II. Herald.
BT732.5 .S8 2015   615.852

Cover design by Jon Ramsey

Contents

Lesson No. 1: Universal Interest in Healing

From earliest times, man has been intent in his search for healing. Disease is at least as old as the Fall of Man. A study of primitive religions reveals that as long as five thousand years ago health and disease were believed to depend on states of the mind. It was assumed that a mental state of reverence for, and fear of, a god brought health; while indifference or hostility to the deity resulted in disease.

Hence, the use of non-physical methods to combat disease is very ancient. Astrologers, sorcerers, and magicians in ancient Egypt, Babylonia, Chaldea, Arabia, Judea, Greece, and Rome believed in the efficacy of charms and incantations, of strange concoctions, and of religious rites for purposes of healing.

In the ancient world the god of healing was Aesculapius. The two great centers of his worship were Rome and Epidaurus. Epidaurus has been called the Lourdes of the ancient world. Sufferers came to these temples, and spent the night there in the darkness. The emblem of Aesculapius is the snake. Accordingly, tame and harmless snakes were let loose in the dormitories; when they touched the people lying there, the people thought that it was the touch of the god and they were healed.

Hippocrates, born about 460 B.C. is generally honored as "The Father of Medicine." He believed that diseases have natural causes and should be treated accordingly. In his medical practice he was cautious, trusting chiefly the operations of nature, and the effects of diet and regimen. As to surgery he followed the maxim that "what cannot be cured by medicine must be cured by the knife; what cannot be cured by the knife must be cured by fire." He classified the fluids or humors of the body as blood, phlegm, black bile, and yellow bile; the right combination of which resulted in health, and any disturbance of which caused disease.

In the Graeco-Roman world, into which Jesus was born, the doctor was held in high esteem. It is from Greece that we get the famous Hippocratic oath, the oath taken originally by Greek doctors before they entered upon the practice of medicine, and the oath which to this day governs medical ethics and practice.

The story of medicine and its amazing discoveries and achievements during the Christian centuries is a dramatic revelation of the universal concern for healing. Every student of the Church's ministry of healing ought to peruse at least a general outline of the history of medicine.

The healing ministry of Jesus Christ, as recorded in the New Testament gospel records, and the regular ministry of healing in the early Church, as revealed in both canonical books, are highly significant confirmations of the unrelenting concern of persons for healing. In subsequent lessons we shall look in more detail at both the healing ministries of Jesus and of the early Church.

The healing ministry was prominent in the Christian Church until the beginning of the 4th century. With the rapid institutionalization of the Church, after its adoption as the official religion of the empire, the emphasis upon healing under Church auspices became less prominent. In fact, it may be said that as far as the regular ministries of the Church are concerned the healing ministry of the Church waned for more than a thousand years. Nevertheless, during all of this period which we call the Middle Ages, the Church was not left without a healing witness in every century. There were those Christian leaders in each of the centuries who emphasized "the forgotten ministry of healing" and by their participation in it helped to restore it to the normal life of the Church. But they never accomplished their hoped-for purpose on a universal level.

The Reformation period with its emphasis upon the Holy Scriptures made possible a climate more conducive to both belief in and practice of healing within the Church. However, the Reformation-emphasis was so largely theological in its focus that healing activities were limited largely to personal experiences. It is interesting to note in passing that each of the reformers bore witness to some kind of experience in relation to healing.

A real revival of interest in healing on the part of the Church throbbed during the past century. This period has witnessed the rise of cults, most of which have a healing emphasis, and the formation of sectaries within Protestant Christianity which also have included healing in their basic tenets and practices. A large number of the small denominations which have come on the American scene during the past century have had an active healing emphasis.

Let it also be kept in mind that the healing emphasis at least in theory has never been entirely lost at any time in the long history of Roman Catholicism. The Roman Catholic Church has long recognized both material and supernatural powers in healing. The student of healing soon becomes aware of the phenomenon of such a healing center as Lourdes.

This is the century of the discovery of the healing emphasis in the older, larger Protestant denominations. Leaders and healing movements are now to be found in most of these denominations. Church commissions have been formed to investigate and report on the healing ministry of the Church. A large number of local churches now carry on regular healing ministries.

Why is there an unusual contemporary interest in the Church's ministry of healing? Let me venture five answers in response to this inquiry:

1. The focus upon the possibility of the healing of the person is an antidote to the alarming and increasing trend of depersonalization in the contemporary age, particularly in industrial and scientific pursuits.

2. There is a growing concern for the total person. Man is clearly seen as a unity. The influence of the component parts of the person upon one another is increasingly manifest. Contemporary medical science is concerned about "the medicine of the person." Wholeness is no longer compartmentalized; it relates to the total person.

3. Within the Church there is a quickened concern about its total ministry. The contemporary Church is re-discovering that it must minister according to the pattern of Jesus' ministry and that of the early Church-preaching, teaching, healing.

4. There is concerned and diligent investigation of the spiritual impetus which undergirds the growing ministries of so many active healing groups both within and outside the Protestant Christian frameworks.

5. There is growing sensitivity to the total needs of people in this contemporary age. There has never been a time when so many people needed some kind of healing. Hosts of people are burdened, bored, tired, nervous, physically ill, emotionally upset, and lacking in spiritual wholeness. There is conscientious concern that persons everywhere discover authentic healing for their many ills.

QUESTIONS FOR DISCUSSION

1. Is interest in and concern for health always a sign of normality within a person?

2. What are some of the healing miracles in the Old Testament?

3. Why did Jesus devote so much time to a ministry of healing?

4. What contacts have you had with healing and/or a healing ministry?

5. Is your church a healing church?

Lesson No. 2: What We Mean By Healing

Let us begin by arriving at a proper designation of the particular activity we are talking about. Healing has been labeled in various ways: "Faith Healing," "Divine Healing," "Christian Healing," "Spiritual Healing."

Even though these are all valid terms and express an aspect of the total truth I believe that each of the terms is too restrictive in relation to the total healing ministry.

Faith healing usually implies the activity of a faith healer. Too frequently the focus is centered upon a person who appears to have a particular gift of healing. The result is that a person's faith becomes dependent upon his personal proximity to such a person and upon the faith healer's activity on his behalf. Even though faith is an essential in the process of healing it can be a distinct hindrance to healing when such faith is in any way dependent upon a human channel of God's healing power rather than upon God Himself who is the Source of all healing

Divine healing is too general a term. All healing is of God. ALL healing is divine. The danger in the use of this term is that we tend to fall back on the arbitrary sovereignty of God in relation to the release of His healing power and as a result often bypass the opportunities of a concentrated healing ministry. Certainly we believe that God's healing power is released in response to intercessory prayer as well as the result of HIS own arbitrary sovereignty.

The term *Christian healing*, although it signifies Jesus Christ as the Great Physician, may give the wrong impression that only Christians can be healed through a healing ministry. The record of healing proves the contrary. The possibility of healing is a universal reality and transcends religious boundaries. However, in fairness to the healing ministries of many of us, it must be said that our prior concern is always that the person seeking healing come into right relationship with and through Jesus Christ.

The term *spiritual healing* is used popularly, though I think mistakenly, to refer to the total ministry of the Church in relation to healing. Actually "spiritual" healing is healing primarily through spiritual means, rather than through physical or psychological methods. "Spiritual" healing is healing through faith, prayer, spiritual disciplines, and the dominance of spiritual values in one's quest for wholeness. Technically, "spiritual" healing means reliance upon meditation instead of medication, aspiration rather than aspirin, consecration more than a clinic.

Certainly there is an overlapping in all of this. Spiritual methods must be actively related to the use of all physical and psychological methods of healing. But it must be said that healing is not limited to spiritual methods alone.

I have come to the conviction that the proper designation of what we are talking about is *the church's ministry of healing*. Since the Church is primarily concerned about wholeness it is interested in every possible healing method to achieve such wholeness.

The Church participates in many ministries - the ministry of worship, of proclamation, of education, of evangelism, of fellowship, of social concern and action. From its institution the Church has also been assigned a ministry of healing. William Barclay writes: "Preaching, teaching, healing - that was the threefold pattern of the ministry of Jesus. Healing was an inseparable part of His work and of the pattern of the work of His apostles."

Jesus' Great Commission to His Church is threefold: "Go teach - go preach - go heal." Dr. Alan Whanger, a medical doctor who has had extensive ministry of the mission field and who is now active in psychiatry in this country, said to me when discussing his interest in the healing ministry: "The Church must engage in this ministry because it is Christ's Commission to the Church."

We move now into the area of an adequate definition. Every student in the field knows that many excellent definitions of healing have been advanced. Let us consider a number of these definitions before discussing the one which will be considered basic in this entire series of lessons.

The following insights are offered by Bernard Martin, minister in Geneva, Switzerland, and a long time leader in the Church's Ministry of Healing:

> "The healing of man is a liberation from physical, mental and spiritual hackles which prevent him from reaching the full maturity of a man destined for eternal life."

"To heal a man includes more than protecting him from destruction. It is also to provide him with the possibility of pursuing his path, to lead him to a progressive blossoming of his person, to return to him the capability of living."

"Sickness is everything which, in one way or another, hinders a man in his path towards the full humanity of Jesus Christ. The healed man therefore is a man in whom the obstacles to the development of his true nature have been eliminated. To be healed means more than to recover the life that one led before falling ill. To be healed means to live normally in every area of one's life."

Evelyn Underhill describes healing in these words:

"Healing is really restoring to the true normality, restoring to full manhood, mending the breaches in our perfect humanity, and making us again what God intends us to be. It shows us His life-giving Spirit; the Lord and Giver of Life ever at work producing and restoring fullness of life. For all disease of soul or body is a subtraction from human nature, a way of being sub-standard. There are no colds in Paradise. So, healing of any sort is a kind of creative or rather regenerating work, a direct expression and furtherance of God's will. It means bringing life back to what it ought to be, mending that which has broken down, healing our deep mental and spiritual wounds by the action of His charity, giving new strength to the weak, new purity to the tainted."

Here are some other meaningful definitions and descriptive statements about healing:

"Healing is the removing of all obstacles to the natural powers resident in us, through the power of God. This 'healing power of nature' is what cures, whatever may be the technique."
                                                    -James D. VanBuskirk

"Healing is directed to man's need for wholeness. Health in the Christian understanding is a continuous and victorious encounter with the powers that deny the existence and goodness of God. It is participation with Christ in an invasion of the realm of evil in which final victory lies beyond death, but the power of that victory is known now in the gift of the life-giving Spirit."
                                                    -T. F. Davey, M.D.

"The purpose of the Commission on Religion and Health is to foster the full evangel of the Church, to preach, teach, and to heal, with special emphasis upon the historical ministry of healing within the Church and its relevance to modern times, and concretely to demonstrate the interrelatedness of modern medicine and vital Christianity, and to implement this through the Sacraments of the Church. Healing is an endeavor to achieve wholeness of mind, body, and spirit within the larger context of a vital Christian faith."

-Commission on Religion and Health,
Protestant Episcopal Church

"Spiritual Healing is God's loving action upon all and every part of our nature."

-Canon Noel Waring

Against the background of the above definitions and descriptive statements let me share the most adequate definition of healing that I have discovered. It is given by Dr. Leslie D.Weatherhead, eminent British clergyman, and a pioneer in the contemporary concern for the Church's Ministry of Healing:

Healing is the process of restoring the broken harmony which prevents human personality, at any point of body, mind, or spirit, from its perfect functioning in its relevant environment; that is, the body in the material world, the mind in the realm of true ideas, and the spirit in its relationship to God.

A study of these definitions reveal some basic truths about healing. First of all, healing relates to normalcy within the person. Healing has as its objective the making possible of the normal functioning of the person on the highest level of being. Weatherhead speaks of "restoring the broken harmony"; Martin speaks of "a liberation from shackles which prevent maturity," "a return to the capability of living," "to live normally in every area of one's life"; Underhill speaks of "making us again what God intends us to be."

In the second place, healing relates to every aspect of the human personality - body, mind, and spirit. Healing is concerned with wholeness for the total person. Sometimes the basic need of a person is for physical healing. At other times the basic need is mental and emotional. Again the basic need is often spiritual. Perhaps there are fundamental needs in more than one area of human personality. Or there may be the need for the harmonious working of all the component parts of the human personality.

The church's ministry of healing rests fundamentally upon the nature of man, as created by God, in His own image. Man has been created as a unity. The basic components of his nature - spirit, mind, and body - are distinct entities and are interrelated, and together they comprise a personality which ideally is characterized by unity. Man fulfills the potential of his creation only as the various parts of his personality work in harmonious balance and effect each other constructively.

Jesus healed persons rather than merely curing diseases. The individual is truly healed in so far as he recovers the possibility of the maturity of his entire person. The healed person is restored and set once again within his true destiny. Healing means wholeness and such wholeness is dependent upon the Holy Spirit's integration of one's total being - body, mind, and spirit.

There is a third truth: healing is usually a process. However, this is not meant to exclude either instantaneous healings or instantaneous acts of faith which initiate healing.

Finally, healing is always purposeful. Healing is never effected for purposes of self-display or even primarily for verbal witnessing. Healing is never to be sought merely as another miracle which the omnipotent God delights to toss about. Rather, healing always relates to the "perfect functioning" of the person. The New Testament concept of "perfect" always includes divine purposefulness. Healing makes possible not only activity in the name of Jesus Christ but also maturity of being in Christ.

QUESTIONS FOR DISCUSSION

1. Why do people tend to restrict their concept of healing to physical healing?

2. Why do people tend to separate what they call "Divine Healing" from healing through natural and scientific means?

3. What is the relation between the salvation Jesus offers and the wholeness of the total person?

4. What is your reaction to the conclusion that "healing is usually a process"?

5. What is your understanding of "a miracle of healing"?

Lesson No. 3: A Biblical Basis for Healing

We begin with healing in the Old Testament. God revealed Himself as Healer. One of the Hebrew names by which God is called is *Jehovah-rapha* - "The Lord who heals" (Exodus 15:26). God gave this revelation of Himself to the Israelites after He saw their plight in Egypt and was purposing to deliver them. God reiterated His healing function as He promised His people, "I will take sickness away from the midst of you" (Exodus 23:25).

Throughout the Old Testament Scriptures healing prayers are addressed to God. "Heal her now, O God, I beseech Thee (Numbers 12:13). "O Lord, heal me" (Psalm 6:2). "Heal me, O Lord, and I shall be healed" (Jeremiah 17:14). Such prayers are grounded in faith in a God who heals. Study Job 2:5; Psalm 103:2,3; Isaiah 53:4,5.

The Bible is replete with stories of healing. (See Nellie B. Woods, *All The Bible Stories of Healing*, Hawthorn Books, Inc.) Space does not permit a detailed listing of the healing miracles in the Old Testament. Suffice it to note some scripture references which may be pursued in personal study:(Genesis 20, Numbers 12:1-16; 21:4-9, I Kings 12:26; 13:10; 17:17-24, II Kings 4:8-37; 5:1-27; 20:1-11, Isaiah 38:1-22, Job 42:1-10, Daniel 4:1-10).

In this regard there are many chapters in the book of the Psalms which have focus and provide valued healing insight. (Study Psalms 6, 23, 32, 38, 39, 51, 62, 88, 91, 100, 103, 116.)

"The Lord who heals" also manifested Himself in prescribing laws of health which when observed became the basic antidotes to sickness and disease. These laws of health which were divinely given may be summarized under six main headings: (1) The law of sanitation (see Exodus 29:14); (2) The law of cleansing (see Leviticus 15); (3) The law of isolation (see Numbers 5 : 1-4); (4) The law of dietetics (see Leviticus 11); (5) The law of personal discipline (see Numbers 6); (6) The law of rest (see Exodus 20:8-1 1 ; Leviticus 25).

S. I. McMillen, M.D. in his book *None Of These Diseases* documents the relationship between the observance of the divinely-given laws of health and the fulfillment of the Divine promises in Exodus 15:26 and 23:25 - "I will put none of these diseases upon you"; "I will take sickness away from the midst of you." The Psalmist testified to the fulfillment of the Divine promise: "There was not one feeble person among their tribes" (Psalm 105:37).

Three truths emerge from a study of healing in the Old Testament:

1. A state of good health was pictured as the ideal situation. The realization of such a state of good health was sometimes impeded by the erroneous Hebrew concept that good health is usually the arbitrary reward of goodness and sickness is the arbitrary judgment for sin.

2. God manifested Himself as One who heals. When healing was manifested it was always considered a Divine work.

3. Wholeness was related to the total person. There was a growing awareness within the Old Testament that wholeness resulted from harmony with God. Throughout the entire Bible a right relationship to God is presented as the ultimate objective.

We move now to the New Testament, and we begin with the life and ministry of Jesus Christ. The Old Testament had predicted that the Coming Messiah would perform a ministry of healing. Isaiah, in the beautiful fifty-third chapter of his recorded prophecy, describes Him as "a man of pains, and acquainted with diseases," as the One who bore our diseases and carried our pains (vs. 3-5 Jewish Version). The New American Bible translates Isaiah 53:5 in this way: "upon Him is the chastisement that makes us whole." Little wonder is it that of the familiar titles of Jesus Christ when He ministered in the flesh was that of a Great Physician.

When Jesus appeared He was a personal demonstration of good health and wholeness. We read in the New Testament scriptures that He was tempted, He became hungry, tired, discouraged, lonely, sad; but never are we told He was ever sick. And the portrait of Him wherever it is found is one of emotional wholeness and of perfect spiritual harmony with His Father.

Jesus' concern for the human body was in line with the best religious thought of his day . He carried on an extensive ministry of healing. In the Gospels, there are records of at least twenty-six healing miracles which Jesus performed upon individuals. There are five other references to His healing ministry in respect to "a great multitude, "many people," and "others."

Any study in depth of the healing ministry of Jesus calls for a detailed consideration of the healing miracles. This would be revelatory of such matters as Jesus' motivation, the extensiveness of His healing power, His healing methods, and His healing words. However, within the limits of this single lesson it is possible merely to note a medical classification of these healing miracles.

Jesus healed the following known ailments: fever, malaria, leprosy, cogenital blindness, Parkinson's disease, nephritis, arthritis, fibroids of the uterus or functional hemorrhage, epilepsy, deafness, blindness, crippledness, and insanity. And certainly Jesus must have encountered also such conditions as the neuroses which are associated with such symptoms as fear, anxiety, insomnia, nervousness, palpitation, heart, disorder, indigestion, excitement, and depression.

When Jesus sent forth His disciples, He instructed them, among other things, to heal the sick. "And when he had' called unto him his twelve disciples, he gave them power against unclean spirits, to cast them out, and to heal all manner of sickness and all manner of disease "(Matthew 10:1).

Many significant summary truths evolve from a study of the healing ministry of Jesus:

1. Jesus devoted much of His ministry to works of healing.

2. When we study the Gospel records it becomes evident that Christ's healing work was on a different level than that of mere human science. We stand in the presence of One who lived on a higher spiritual plan than we normally penetrate. Spiritual energies of immense power were at His disposal.

3. Christ's healing miracles are not the same as mere psychological cures. Scientific research and discoveries are not adequate to release the energies used by Christ.

4. Jesus Christ did not break any established cosmic laws in the effecting of His healing miracles. Weatherhead defines a miracle in this way: "a law-abiding event by which God accomplishes His redemptive purposes through the release of energies which belong to a plane of being higher than any with which we are normally familiar." Or as another has said: "miracles are not contrary to nature, but only contrary to what we know about nature."

5. Jesus' primary motivation in His healing ministry was that of compassion. Because He loved people He wanted them to become whole.

6. The real object of Christ's healing miracles was spiritual and redemptive: through the inflow of God's power into their total beings, to infuse God's truths into men's minds; to pour God's love into men's hearts; to bring men into a right relationship to God.

7. It was inevitable that the healing miracles of Christ's ministry should become signs of the Kingdom He

came to establish. "Heal the sick, and say unto them, the Kingdom of God is come nigh unto you" (Luke 10:11).

As the earthly ministry of Jesus was drawing to a close. He told his disciples that "he that believeth on me, the works that I do shall he do also; and greater works than these shall he do" (John 14:12). In fulfillment of the divine promise and in obedience to the divine command, healing became a regular ministry in the early Christian church. There are records of fourteen healings in the Book of Acts.

The New Testament writers often related the health of the body to the grace of God. Paul writes, "For this cause many are weak and sickly among you" (I Corinthians 11:30), "the body for the Lord and the Lord for the body" (I Corinthians 6: 13).John wrote solicitously: "I wish above all things that thou mayest prosper and be in health, even as thy soul prospereth" (III John 2).

James, in his epistle gives interesting instructions to the sick concerning prayers for healing. "Is any among you afflicted? Let him pray. Is any merry? Let him sing psalms. Is any sick among you? Let him call for the elders of the church; and let them pray over him, anointing him with oil in the name of the Lord: and the prayer of faith shall save the sick, and the Lord shall raise him up; and if he have committed sins, they shall be forgiven him" (5:13-15).

In 1 Corinthians 12, Paul asserts that the gift of healing is one of the gifts of the Holy Spirit that has been given to the Church. The Apostle writes: "But the manifestation of the Spirit is given to every man to profit withal. For to one is given by the Spirit the word of wisdom;

to another the word of knowledge by the same Spirit; to another faith by the same Spirit; to another the working of miracles; to another prophecy; to another discerning of spirits; to another divers kinds of tongues; to another the interpretation of tongues; but all these worketh that one and the selfsame Spirit, dividing to every man severally as he will" (I Corinthians 12:7-11).

The specific gift of healing is to be viewed in the light of these truths concerning spiritual gifts in general: (1)The gifts are charismatic in nature. They are gifts of God's grace. (2) The validity of the gifts is based on Christ's redemptive triumph. (3) The gifts have a common source- the Holy Spirit. (4) There is a distinction between gifts of the Spirit and the Gift of the Spirit. (5) There is a variety of gifts. (6) The distribution of the gifts is in accord with the divine wisdom. (7) The gifts are to be used for "the good of all."

Any discussion of the gift of healing raises an inevitable question: has this spiritual gift of healing, so prominently used in the early Church, ever been withdrawn?

Even though there are those who say that the gift of healing has been withdrawn there does not seem to be any external evidence to support their claim. Rather does it appear that the gift of healing remains the possession of the Church as the body of believers? Even in New Testament times when the gift of healing was evident in the activities of individual Christians, it was given for their use "for the common good." Thus it is logical to believe that the gift of healing now belongs to the whole body of believers, and the contemporary Church under divine inspiration is to carry on an active ministry of healing.

QUESTIONS FOR DISCUSSION

1. What do you think is the connection between one's relationship to God and one's health? Is good health the reward of righteousness? Is sickness the sign of divine judgment?

2. Is the healing power of Jesus relevant to Christians today?

3. How do you react to the idea that in our day perhaps the gift of healing is given primarily to the Church as a group of believers, rather than merely to individuals?

4. Are you convinced that the Bible supports an active ministry of healing in the local church?

Lesson No. 4: A Theology of Healing

A ministry of healing is impossible without an undergirding and sustaining theology. Just what do we mean by "a theology of healing"? Let's begin with the word "theology." It means "the science of God." A "theology" relates to a body of truth dealing with God and his relation to the world. To the theist, a "theology" is a body of truth which is God-oriented, God revealed, and God supported.

"A theology of healing," therefore, relates to those aspects of theological truth which we believe reveal God as supportive of and active in the total healing process. "A theology of healing" assumes our acceptance of a scriptural view of God as creator, of the nature of human creation, and of the activity of the divine creator in the restoration of His creation. "A theology of healing" builds upon our confidence in the authenticity of the divine revelation in the holy scriptures and particularly as this revelation exposes God's desire for and activity in relation to wholeness within the creature and the creation.

There is not a theology of Christian healing *per se*. Such an isolated theology would tend to make healing an end in itself and this could pervert God's purpose into self-centered action. A "theology of healing" grows out of basic

Christian theology. Because of our theology of creation, which views man as created in the image of God; our theology of the kingdom of God, which shows the divine purpose to be the fulfillment of the divine will within the creation; our theology of the Church as a healing community; our theology of the endless life which calls for the final and perfect restoration of man, there emerges for us a satisfying "theology of healing."

Let it be stated briefly and summarily that only an adequate theology will impel one to dedicated and persistent spiritual being and doing. Even though we may not always be quick to identify such a causal relationship it takes a theology of prayer for us to pray, a theology of love for us to love and serve, a theology of spiritual experience for us to worship and witness, a theology of the Church for us to be good churchmen, a theology of truth and holiness for us to be ethical. Just so, an adequate undergirding theology of healing is needed for participation in the Church's ministry of healing. In the last analysis we will not act in a healing ministry unless we are motivated and supported by a theology which is a basic part of our religious faith.

Let me share with you the five basic tenets in my "theology of healing:"

I. *The human creature, in the varied aspects and manifestations of his person, has intrinsic and eternal value.* First of all, the total person has intrinsic value. The holy scriptures reveal man as created in the image of God - a rational, moral, spiritual image. God passed His highly favorable verdict upon His creation. "And God saw everything that He had made, and, behold, it was very good" (Gen. 1:31).

The incarnation of Jesus Christ reveals the intrinsic worth of the total person. "Jesus increased in wisdom and stature, and in favor with God and man" (Luke 2:52). Throughout His ministry Jesus was concerned about the total man-his physical, mental, emotional, spiritual "hurts."

In a more particular sense the human body has intrinsic value. The Old Testament reveals this in its picture of the divine creation, in its revelation of the levitical laws to safeguard health, and its relating physical and spiritual health to its concept of salvation.

The incarnate Christ appeared in a human body and "dwelt among us" (John 1:14). The ministry of the incarnate Christ revealed the concern of Jesus Christ for the human body. His miracles of healing upon the body were so numerous that He was known as the Great Physician.

The New Testament scriptures speak of the body being redeemed (I Cor. 6:20); being justified, sanctified, washed (I Cor. 6:11); being a member of Christ (I Cor. 6:15); being indwelt by the Holy Spirit (I Cor. 6:19); belonging to God (I Cor. 6:19); and ultimately being raised up (I Cor. 6:14). Little wonder is it that the apostle Paul exhorts us to glorify God in our bodies (I Cor. 6:20).

II. God wills wholeness for every person. I do not believe that God wills sin or sickness or accident or affliction. Rather I do believe that God wills that every person be whole in every aspect of his being and that such wholeness in body, in mind, and in soul be harmonized in a total personality wholeness. Let me share in a summary manner the reasons why I believe that God wills wholeness for every person.

1. God's purpose for His creatures as expressed in the original creation is seen to be that of wholeness. The original creation was perfect. The scriptures tell us that God said it was "good, very good." The way God created man originally must have been the way He wanted him to be always. Thus, any lack of wholeness in man is the result of man's sin rather than the purpose of God.

2. God has made us with built-in, automatic powers of healing. Within us are the always abiding processes of recuperation and restoration with which we cooperate in all healing.

3. The Old Testament prophets had insights into God's purposeful wholeness. At times in the Old Testament writings the terms "salvation" and "health" are used almost interchangeably.

4. The perfect health of Jesus Christ, the incarnate Son of God, is a revelation of "the glory of humanity" expressed through the possibility of wholeness. Even though Jesus was tempted and tried, there is no record of His being sick. Certainly one result of the incarnation is to reveal "the glory of humanity," a revelation of what humanity could have been if sin had not entered.

5. Think also of the healing ministry of Jesus. The healing ministry of Jesus was in partial fulfillment of His redemptive objective: "I am come that you might have life, and have it abundantly." The Gospel records reveal dramatically that wherever Jesus Christ touched human life He restored wholeness.

6. The divine commission to the Church reveals God's will that men should be whole. Jesus commissioned His disciples to teach and preach and heal. The gift of healing was one of the gifts of the Holy Spirit imparted to the early church. Was this merely mockery, or was it rather a charismatic confirmation of the divine intention that men should be whole? Students of apostolic and post-apostolic times affirm that the early church had a regular ministry of healing.

7. Are we willing to write off the significant influences of the Church's ministry of healing through the centuries as outside the will of God? What about hospitals under Christian auspices? What about medical missions? What about deeply committed medical researchers and practicing physicians? What about miracles of healing through the centuries? What about the phenomenal rise of the Church's ministry of healing in our day?

8. Finally, the contemporary medical emphasis upon "the medicine of the person" is a scientific confirmation of the divine intention of wholeness. Physicians know that the total person must be healed if any part of the person is to be healed fully. The human being is all of one piece, and physical and spiritual attitudes can not be treated independently. Either man is treated in his wholeness as a human being or he is not really treated. Today's education of the future physician emphasizes personal and social values as well as scientific knowledge and abilities.

III. Salvation and wholeness are intimately related: you cannot separate them. Here let me quote from three authorities

- a philosopher, a theologian, and a leader in the church's ministry of healing:

> "Salvation means wholeness, deliverance from all that injures or mutilates, or hinders the growth of the personality. It means fullness of life, well-being, strength, power, blessedness, wealth, happiness, righteousness, joy, peace. It is the complete penetration of the human by the divine."
>
> -William E. Hocking

> "But the point is that the very word 'salvation' means 'health.' In the original Greek *soteria*, which we translate as 'salvation,' can also denote a healthy condition. In Latin, *salus*, which we also translate as 'salvation,' has the related meaning of 'health.' In Anglo-Saxon languages the same is true: *heil* and *heilig* in German mean 'healthy' and 'holy'; and in our own tongue, 'whole' and 'holy,' 'hale' and 'holiness,' have the same root. This seems to me very significant, for it shows that there is some deep instinct in man which intimately relates his actual health as a human being with a relationship with others and with God, which is sound and right and acceptable."
>
> -Norman Pittenger

> "Jesus Christ speaks to man as a whole. He is not careful to distinguish between moral and physical states. The redemption He preached is a redemption of the whole man, body, soul, and spirit."

-Alfred W. Price

IV. All healing is of God. The healing power belongs to God. Medicine does not heal. Doctors and surgeons do not heal. Psychiatric therapies do not heal. Rest does not heal. Climate does not heal. God only uses these means and agents of healing. All of these become opportunities for God to heal.

These words of the eminent French doctor, Ambroise Pare, are inscribed over the gateway of the College of Surgeons in Paris- "I dressed the patient's wounds; God healed him." Over the entrance to the Columbia-Presbyterian Medical Center in New York City are these words- "For from the Most High cometh healing."

Ernest White, M. D., psychologist of Harley Street, London, England, says: "We believe that the gift of healing, whether in the realm of medicine or surgery on the physical plane, or of psychotherapy on the mental plane, comes ultimately from God."

In his volume *A Place For You*, Paul Tournier, M. D. says that he thinks one of the reasons why people come to him to be treated is because he is weak and they believe he is relying on God rather than on his own efforts. He writes: "I know well that there is not much that I have done, but that it is the work of God."

I must add one further brief word in this section. I do not believe that devils can heal. I am reminded of what was spoken after Jesus healed a blind man: "How could a demon open the eyes of a blind man?" (John 10:21). Satan's purpose is to keep persons from wholeness and to rob them of it. Jesus Christ came that men might have life and have it abundantly (John 10:10).

V. The fifth aspect of my "theology of healing" is the conviction that *there is a vital relationship between the Christian Faith and healing.* This truth is so important and deserves such careful documentation that I am reserving my discussion of it for the next lesson (No. 5) in the School of Healing.

QUESTIONS FOR DISCUSSION

1. Discuss the statement that "every thinking person is a theologian of one kind or another."

2. Why is there a tendency among some religious people (including Christians) to depreciate the human body?

3. What is the relation of "the will of God" to such things as sin, sickness, accident, calamity, death?

4. Study Isaiah 53. What does this chapter teach about the relationship between salvation and health?

Lesson No. 5: The Relation Between the Christian Faith and Healing

Actually this is a continuation of the last lesson. In view of the fact that this lesson deals with the fifth and final basic tenet in my "theology of healing," before discussing it let me reiterate the other four.

First, the human creature, in the varied aspects and manifestations of his person, has intrinsic and eternal value. Second, God wills wholeness for every person. Third, salvation and wholeness are intimately related; you cannot separate them. Fourth, all healing is of God.

In this lesson we will discuss in detail the relationship which exists between the Christian faith and healing. I want to present a five-fold relationship, the discovery of which really embarked me on my healing ministry more than two decades ago. During all these intervening years of careful study and active participation in the field of healing, these convictions have remained steadfast and have been repeatedly and progressively confirmed.

1. To begin with, the Christian faith inspires healthy living and this is the best prevention of disease. Just suppose

an individual from his early life really lived the Christian way - would not healthy living result in most instances and much sickness be avoided?

Dr. James Van Buskirk in his volume *Religion, Healing, and Health*, reminds us that there are nine characteristics of the Christian way of life, all of which contribute to a person's health. Christianity teaches and encourages the proper care of the body. It enforces the virtue of honest work, which has a definite therapeutic value. The Christian faith promotes recreation and relaxation. It encourages a person to turn from himself and to rest in the Lord. Christianity encourages Christian worship, which also has a therapeutic effect. It encourages the study of the Bible, allowing its constructive power to operate upon the personality. The Christian gospel offers faith as the only antidote to fear, and it frees the human personality from the devastating burden of guilt. Jesus Christ always says "forgive," "love one another."

2. There is a second relationship between the Christian faith and healing. The Christian faith is able to aid healing through physical and psychological methods by the creation of the proper mental, emotional, and spiritual attitudes within the patient. This is clearly demonstrated in what is commonly known as "the will to live."

Negatively considered, there are case records of what are called "psychological deaths." There are patients who lose interest in life, and feeling that there is nothing worth living for, they succumb to the first illness that comes along. And even when death does not result, the process of physical or mental recovery is impeded drastically and prolonged by wrong attitudes.

Positively speaking, it is this "will to live" which is often the deciding factor between death and recovery. An anesthetist said: "Patients who go to the operating table with a confident faith in God take less anesthetic, recover from it more easily and with far less of the usual distressing aftereffects."

3. To make the analysis accurate, there is a third relationship that should be mentioned. There have been times when the Church's ministry of healing and medical science have joined hands to effect a healing, each contributing something to the healing that the other could not.

There is the record of the young boy in South Africa who needed a brain operation, but was subject to blackouts. The brain surgeon in Johannesburg said that he could not operate until the boy had been free of blackouts for six months. In desperation the parents took their son to Mrs. Elsie Salmon, the wife of a Methodist minister, who has had a remarkable ministry of healing. After eight months, the boy had experienced no blackouts. They returned him to the surgeon in Johannesburg. The operation was performed. It was one of the earliest operations on record where they removed a sphere of the brain. The operation was a success and the young man became one of the outstanding artists in South Africa.

Now what had happened? The Church's ministry of healing did something and medical science did something to make possible the healing. Each made a contribution which the other did not make. Certainly this is being confirmed in our day as a rapidly developing and increasingly effective relationship between medical science and spiritual healing.

4. We come now to the fourth relationship between the Christian faith and healing. The Christian faith is able to direct the healing of all those functional illnesses which have been caused by wrong mental, emotional, and/or spiritual attitudes.

There is a difference between an organic or structural illness and a functional illness. In an organic or structural illness something is wrong with the nature of the organ or body structure itself. A functional illness is one in which there is nothing inherently wrong, but an organ or a bodily structure is malfunctioning. And what is the cause? The answer is clear: wrong mental attitudes, negative emotions, improper spiritual relationships within a person. Doctors now estimate that 75-80 percent of all sickness is functional in nature. This is what is known as psychosomatic illness.

How devastating is the effect of wrong mental attitudes, negative emotions, and improper spiritual relationships upon the total person. Every negative emotion, except the normal expression of grief, is destructive. Such things as fear, anxiety, ill will, guilt, inferiority, and negativism are destructive in their effect upon the human personality.

Dr. Blaine E. McLaughlen, director of psychiatry at Women's Medical College, Philadelphia, says that 60 to 85 percent of all patients in doctors' offices have psychosomatic complaints. He says that 99percent of all headaches, 75 percent of all gastric upsets, 75 percent of skin diseases, and 85 percent of all asthma cases are psychosomatic in nature.

A doctor who attended the medical needs of a General Motors plant in a certain city said: "Seventy-five percent of the executives of this plant have gastric ulcers due to the pressures upon them to succeed or be replaced."

Dr. Karl Meiminger says: "Guilt changes the physical structure of the body and makes the person more susceptible to disease."

Dr. John W. Keyes, a heart specialist of the Henry Ford Hospital in Detroit, Michigan, speaking at a meeting of the American Medical Association in Miami Beach, Florida, declared that some heart disease may be imaginary, brought on by the patient's fears and his doctor's words or attitudes. Dr. Keyes explained: "The patients may have symptoms ranging from chest pains to dizziness, from fatigue to palpitations. Once symptoms of this type have occurred, they of themselves can produce a vicious cycle of anxiety which convinces the patient that heart disease is actually present."

Thus it is evident that the effective way to deal with functional illnesses is to deal with the basic causes. Something radical must be done.

The mind must be disciplined away from wrong mental attitudes and into the direction of positive, constructive, authentic thinking. Negative emotions must be replaced by positive emotions. Fear must be replaced by faith; anxiety by confidence. Ill will must give way to genuine love. The guilt-ridden must find true forgiveness. Inferiority attitudes must be supplanted by a sense of adequacy through spiritual resources. Negativism must be rejected as an anti-Christian attitude.

All spiritual relationships must be rectified and developed in the light of the teachings and example of Jesus Christ.

Putting it all together it would appear that in these areas the basic healing is achieved through the power of Jesus Christ actively at work in and through human faculties. The power of Jesus Christ becomes effective continually in the disciplined conscious life and through the working of the Holy Spirit in the subconscious life of the fully dedicated person.

5. The final aspect of the relationship between the Christian faith and healing is healing by the direct activity of God apart from the use of intermediary psychological or physical methods. Human experience bears eloquent testimony to healing by the direct touch of God after human skill has been unable to go any further, after physical and psychological methods have exhausted themselves. When we speak of healing by the direct activity of God, we refer to God intervening directly in a person's experience, apart from all recognizable human sources of remedy and cure, bringing to the individual healing that is clearly demonstrable, at the place of the mind, or soul, or body, or in a combination of any two of these areas of human personality, or of all three areas.

Such healings are easily identified as "miracles of healing." God does something which would not have been accomplished without His intervention. You and I would never have known some of the "great hearts of the faith" if God has not intervened in their experience with such miracles of healing. I think at once among others of E. Stanley Jones, Catherine Marshall (now Le-Sourd), Albert Cliffe, and Oral Roberts.

I think of the late Dwight Eisenhower, in whose youth a healing miracle spared his leg from amputation. And certainly all of us think of relatives and friends whom God healed with His direct touch. May I add that one of the thrilling chapters in the life of the institution I represent is the story of the healing ministry on campus and the resulting healings in the lives of students and staff and related persons.

Thus, we have completed two lessons dealing with "a theology of healing." We end by repeating the convictions with which we began. Only an adequate theology will impel us to dedicated and continuing spiritual activity. Therefore, a ministry of healing is impossible without an undergirding and sustaining theology. In the last analysis we will act in a healing ministry only as we are motivated and supported by a theology of healing, a basic part of our religious faith.

QUESTIONS FOR DISCUSSION

1. Should we try to achieve a balance between an emphasis upon theology and upon experience in the life of the local church? If so, how do we proceed to do it?

2. Does the average evangelical Christian accept as a part of "gospel preaching" sermons on health and healing?

3. Is there a difference in "the exercise of faith" in relation to healing primarily through physical means and healing primarily through spiritual methods?

4. How can the local church encourage greater cooperation between its own ministry of healing and medical science in its various branches?

Lesson No. 6: The Healing Steps

God is a God of plan and order. This is an orderly universe. God's laws are continually in operation. The cosmos is sustained through such divine orderliness. Henry Drummond reminds us that "nothing that happens in this world happens by chance. God is a God of order. Everything is arranged upon definite principles, and never at random. The world, even the religious world, is governed by law."

The Christian experiences are governed by law. If a person wishes to be saved there are certain steps which must be taken. There are also well defined steps in receiving the fullness of the Holy Spirit. Prayers are answered, divine guidance is received, character is achieved, as a result of cooperation with the divine laws which have been revealed in the holy scriptures.

E. D. Starbuck, eminent psychologist, declares: "There is no event in the spiritual life which does not occur in accordance with immutable laws."

Just so, God's healing, through any of the various healing methods, is to be sought along a clearly marked path. The healing process is not magical or irrational. There are definite healing steps to be taken by the person seeking healing.

Our lesson today discusses six such healing steps. It cannot be established precisely that these steps must be taken in the order in which they are discussed. In the light of personal circumstances it could well be that there is a different succession of the steps in some instances. However, it can be affirmed that sometime in the healing process every one of the steps, and the spiritual stage which each represents, must be experienced.

1. RELAXATION

The first step is that of relaxation. "Be still and know that I am God" (Ps. 46:10). A literal Hebrew translation of the above verse is "Relax and discover that I am God." The word "relaxation" means "to be loose again." The opposite of relaxation is tension. In seeking healing the body must be relaxed and freed of all tension. In fact, the body must be "forgotten" so that the mind can concentrate on God and on His healing power.

Alfred W. Price exhorts the one seeking healing in these words: "Relax your body and mind so that all tension goes out of you. We cannot truly contact God except in stillness. One does not go before the King with a torrent of words. Love offers itself to Him, and prayer becomes a sacrifice, not a demand. . .Bring to mind some of His bold affirmations, such as the prophetic word: 'in quietness and confidence shall be your strength' (Isa. 30:15)."

There must be a soul-relaxation. "Be still, and know that I am God." Having attained an attitude of stillness, the greatest of all thoughts will then come stealing into one's mind. We then know that "I am God"- that God is the One who is at work, that God is the One who does the healing. A marginal reading of Psalm 62:5 states: "My soul, be thou silent unto God." Oswald Chambers describes this silence as that which springs from the absolute certainty that God knows what He is doing.

2. PURGING

The second step is that of purging. "If we walk in the light as he is in the light, we have fellowship one with another, and the blood of Jesus Christ his Son cleanseth us from all sin" (I Jn. 1:7). The subconscious mind must be cleansed of all wrong emotions and sinful states, so that the healing power of God can flow through it. There must be the consciousness of divine forgiveness in the soul. God's healing power can work only in those who are living in accord with His laws. "Blessed are the pure in heart: for they shall see God" (Matt. 5:8). A person must rid himself of anything and everything that would keep God from working effectively in his life.

James Denney helps us to understand what it means "to walk in the light": (1) to confess our sins without reserve, never to explain, extenuate, or excuse them; (2) to accept our responsibility without reserve for our sins; (3) to refuse to keep a secret hold on our sins in our hearts after we have confessed them to God and received His forgiveness.

Much time can be wasted in praying for people who cannot or will not confess their sins. If the sick one will not be reconciled to just one other person, prayer may be quite ineffectual. If one does not "leave there thy gift and go and be reconciled. . ." prayer will not help. If the sick one has some bitter grief, or sense of injustice which he cannot share, God cannot help until it comes out. The sick person may not be committing outward sins, but may be experiencing some wrong attitude or unwholesome state of mind or soul which may seem justifiable to him because of the circumstances involved.

3. CLARIFICATION

The third step is that of clarification. "And Jesus stood still, and called [the blind men] and said. What do you want me to do for you?" (Matt. 20:32). The response of the blind men was immediate and specific. They did not say: "Anything You want to do for us," or "Help us to have a good feeling." They answered at the point of their deepest physical need: "That our eyes may be opened."

The person seeking healing must not be vague or general. He must be specific, telling God exactly the area in which he needs healing. He must visualize exactly his need and vocalize specifically his desire.

We must be sure of the area in which we need healing. Some people are not sick, they are only tired. They need rest. Some people are not sick, they only think they are sick. They need mental discipline. When we know the area of our need of healing then we are to present our request clearly and specifically to the Great Physician.

4. CONSECRATION

The fourth step is that of consecration. "Whether we live therefore, or die, we are the Lord's"(Rom. 14:8). One of the conditions of divine healing is this spiritual attitude of the absolute relinquishment of one's life to the will of God. There must be complete surrender to God on the part of the person seeking divine healing. If the will of God be that health is restored immediately, then let God be praised. If health cannot be restored at once, then let the seeker realize that God is in every human circumstance and that ultimately His purpose will be made manifest. Just so, the seeker must be characterized by a sincere willingness to glorify God and to live for others.

When we really take the step of consecration we do not have to include in our healing prayers the words "if it be Thy will." We have settled that matter. We are the Lord's when sick. We are the Lord's as we seek healing. We will be the Lord's, whatever the consequences.

Jesus insisted on a positive faith: "When you pray, what things you desire, believe that you receive them, and you shall have them" (Mk. 11:24). "If you shall ask anything in my name, I will do it" (Jn. 14:14). Hence, when we pray for healing, we must not make any reservation by adding "If it be Thy will." Jesus never taught that the will of God was ever against healing. But He did teach that unbelief could stand in the way of healing. Therefore, all "ifs" must be excluded from prayers for healing.

5. ANTICIPATION

The fifth step, and indeed a strategic step, is that of anticipation. This is the step of faith. "Faith is the substance of things hoped for, the evidence of things not seen" (Hebrews 11:1). As one seeks healing there must be an eager expectancy, the attitude of an active faith. Never must a seeker think in terms of failure. Always there is the anticipation of God fulfilling what He has already promised.

In his discussion of faith and its relation to healing. Albert E. Day in his book, *An Autobiography Of Prayer*, gives a practical analysis of what is involved in an active faith. Among other things he reminds us that faith is the acceptance of a thing as beneficial - for illustration, the employment of prayer to effect healing. Faith is also the reception of an idea as true - for example, the idea that healing power is available. Faith is, likewise, the acceptance of a personality as real - to illustrate, one's own personality as a psychosomatic reality, subject to spiritual laws as well as physical; and God's personality as Master of both the physical and spiritual realms.

Thus faith means absolute fidelity to all these ideas: a fidelity which manifests itself in a certain quality of life - living by prayer, living in quest for and in acceptance of the healing. Life giving power, living as if spiritual laws were as important as physical laws, living as if God were Master in both areas and would demonstrate His mastery if one will give Him the required cooperation.

In seeking healing there must always be the spirit of anticipation. One is reminded of what we read in the Gospels about certain of the healings performed by Jesus. On more than one occasion the person was healed in the same hour that belief was exercised. "His servant was healed in the selfsame hour" (Matt. 8:13). "Her daughter was made whole from that very hour" (Matt. 15:28). "Yesterday at the seventh hour the fever left him. So the father knew that it was at the same hour, in the which Jesus said unto him, thy son liveth..."(Jn. 4:52, 53).

Certainly it becomes evident that when these five healing steps have been taken - relaxation, purging, clarification, consecration, anticipatory faith - there has been created what Emily Gardiner Neal describes as "the power climate for healing." Like all the rest of God's creative processes, the proper climate is necessary for life and growth, for "new life," and the manifestation of all the "quickening powers of God's Spirit."

6. APPROPRIATION

The final and climatic healing step is that of appropriation. "I can do all things through Christ who gives me strength" (Phil. 4:13). The seeker receives what God has promised, begins acting in the strength of the healing power received, and is grateful to God for the reality of the healing power in his life. "Father, I thank Thee," is the consummation of the personal appropriation of the divine blessings.

QUESTIONS FOR DISCUSSION

1. How can a person learn to "relax" in the scriptural sense of "relaxation"?

2. How can a person discover accurately the area or areas of his/her need of healing?

3. Distinguish between the kinds of prayers that must include the words "if it be Thy will" and those that do not require such a reservation.

4. What are the factors that encourage anticipatory faith? What are the hindrances to anticipatory faith?

Lesson No. 7: How to be Healed

E. Stanley Jones has reminded us of seven ways by which God heals:

1.   God heals through surgeons. Medical history is replete with cases where individuals have been healed as the result of an operation.

2.   God heals through physicians. God has laid up in nature various remedies which medical science is in the process of discovering. Such remedies are to be used wisely, but never overused or abused.

3.   God can heal through mental suggestions. A person can suggest sickness to himself and he will become sick. On the other hand, you can think health, and talk health to yourself, and it aids the healing process. How often healing through physical and psychological methods has been aided by constructive mental, emotional, and spiritual attitudes within the patient.

4.   God can heal through climate. Although this can be overstressed- for the real climate of health or ill health is within a person - nevertheless some

climates are more conducive to health and some are more conducive to disease.

5. God heals through a person's deliverance from underlying fears, loneliness, self-centeredness, purposelessness, resentments, and guilts, which produce disease.

6. God heals through the direct operation of the Spirit of God up on the body. There is no nerve or tissue which is beyond the healing touch of the Spirit of God.

7. God also heals through the final cure - the resurrection of the body. Some diseases must await the final cure in the resurrection. This does not mean that God will not heal. Rather, it means that He has postponed healing for some, to await the final cure in the resurrection of the body. He will heal later on. In the meantime He gives the sufferer power not merely to bear his suffering but to use it, until the final release.

Against this background of the various ways in which God heals, and keeping in mind that six of the seven ways relate to us in our mortal existence, let us consider the question "How can a person be healed?" What guidelines can be given to a person who is seeking healing? For the sake of clarity and convenience let me attempt an answer in a more or less outline form.

The basic step, and an absolutely essential one in healing, is for a person to discover whether he/she is actually sick.

I. Some persons are not actually sick - they only think they are sick.

A doctor said of one man: "For forty years Tom has suffered agonies from imaginitis, scarcoma, apprehenditis, and general fearosis of living."

If a person only thinks that he is sick, then he must be helped to discipline his thoughts in the direction of health, vitality, and adequate strength in Jesus Christ.

II. Some persons are not actually sick - they are only tired.

If it is physical tiredness, then the cure is rest. Some of the healing movements have prescribed "rest treatments." A body will recuperate from mere physical tiredness in twenty-four to forty-eight hours. But there are many other things that cause fatigue: inner guilt, oversensitivity, self-centeredness, boredom, fear, worry, indecision, inferiorities, and resentments.

III. But suppose a person is actually sick. How do you know whether you are actually sick? In the same way that you can know you are healed: by the verdict of medical science in relation to physical and mental/emotional sickness and by the verdict of the spiritual counselor in the case of spiritual sickness.

Sickness can affect any part of the human personality: body, mind, emotions, soul. If the body is sick, physical health must be restored. If the mind or emotions are sick, mental health must be achieved. If the soul is basically sick, out of harmony with God and in wrong relation to others, then holiness must be sought and begun.

BODILY SICKNESS

There are two types of bodily sickness: functional and organic or structural. A functional illness is one in which even though there is nothing wrong with the organs or structure of the body they are malfunctioning because of wrong attitudes or emotions within the person. Doctors estimate conservatively that 75% of all illnesses are functional. On the other hand, an organic or structural illness is the result of something wrong with an organ or structure of the body.

Here are suggested steps in dealing with bodily sickness:

- If the sickness is functional in both manifestation and cause then it must be dealt with mentally, emotionally, and spiritually. Such destructive emotions as guilt, self-centeredness, fear, anxiety, worry, resentments, hatred, ill will, and inferiorities, which cause functional illness, must be brought to the level of the conscious mind, confessed, and replaced by positive emotions (their opposites) made possible through the grace of Jesus Christ.

- If the illness has distinctly organic or structural manifestations, but has been caused by functional disturbances, physical methods should be employed to remedy the organic or structural maladies that are present. Then spiritual methods must be used to remove the basic causes of such organic or structural manifestations.

- If the illness is distinctly organic or structural in both manifestation and cause, all reasonable, normal physical and psychological methods should be employed.

Reputable physicians and surgeons should be consulted and their mature advice followed. Proved medical methods and treatments should be utilized. Psychiatrists who operate within a Christian frame of reference should be permitted to give their diagnosis and prescribe their remedies.

But what if reasonable and normal physical and psychological methods, even when used prayerfully, prove to be ineffective and the person is not healed? I believe that it is at this point that there is the opportunity for a person to seek healing through direct divine activity. (See Lesson No. 5 "The Relation between the Christian Faith and Healing.")

It is in such cases that a healing service is deeply meaningful and strategic. (Healing services will be discussed in a subsequent lesson.)

MENTAL-EMOTIONAL SICKNESS

Whenever there is clearly indicated mental and emotional sickness, a trained professional should be consulted. In such cases scientific help is needed. But let it be kept in mind that mere psychological analysis is not adequate for healing. Such analysis may help a person to understand both the nature and cause of his illness, but in itself it cannot provide healing. To use a term that has been popularized by Dr. Alfred W. Price, the International Warden of the Order of St. Luke the Physician, the person needs psychosynthesis as well as psycho-analysis. People are made well in their minds and emotions and nerves only as Jesus Christ effects a harmonious working relationship between the various parts of their personality.

SPIRITUAL SICKNESS

The essence of spiritual sickness is the estrangement of the person from God. This estrangement is caused by self-centeredness, putting one's self in the place of God. Hence, the refusal to yield one's self to the authority of God and to the lordship of Jesus Christ. The cure for spiritual sickness is confession of sin and a total submission of one's self to God, who has revealed Himself in and through Jesus Christ.

What, then, is the process of "being made whole" in one's soul? Let the person seeking such wholeness of soul express it this way:

"I need to be made whole. I confess my sins, particularly my sin of self-centeredness. I accept Jesus Christ as my savior from sin and as the one who is able to make me whole at the center of my being. I submit to the lordship of Jesus Christ in my daily life. I gladly witness to others concerning the new life of wholeness which Jesus Christ has effected within me."

In the seeking of healing in any area of the human personality the healing steps are of supreme importance. (Review again Lesson No. 6 "The Healing Steps.")

As we seek healing we must meditate upon the healing presence of God. We must remind ourselves that God is present, and that His presence is a loving presence, a healing presence. In the stillness of God's presence we enter more deeply into the realization of His love and power. Because God loves us we know that we can entrust ourselves

- body, mind, emotions, soul, will, - into the healing power of His presence.

Into God's hands, therefore, we surrender the keys of our total being, that He may unlock every door and by His spirit enter into every chamber and possess us with His healing presence. God within brings love, joy, peace, and power.

The Very Rev. Claude O'Flaherty, M.D., has given a meaningful and moving description of what happens when every part of a person is possessed by the healing presence (*Sharing Magazine*, April 1972):

WILL

"He enters the chamber of my will. I surrender it unto His hands, and He sets it truly. As the needle of the compass is set to point to the North, so He sets my will true, to point in line with the Father's will, so that the will of God can flow through mine undeflected to its accomplishment. I will what God wills."

MEMORY

"He enters into the chamber of my memory and fills it with His light and love. He opens all the cupboards and sees all that is past, all that I remember, all that I have forgotten, and all that I have never known. As I confess my sins. He deals with them in His love. His forgiveness cleanses me from all sin, and breaks the power of sinful habit."

AFFECTIONS

"He enters into the chamber of my affection. I give them into His power. He disentangles my desires from all that is unworthy of the child of God, and sets my affections truly on things above, on all that is good and joyous and well pleasing in God's sight."

UNDERSTANDING

"He enters the chamber of my understanding and fills me with that deep inner knowledge of God, which is eternal life – knowledge too deep for the intellect to grasp, the knowledge of growing intimacy."

BODY

"As He fills my mind. He fills the organ of my mind, my brain and nervous system. Every nerve comes to rest in His peace. . .As the nerves rest, they are refreshed, restored and recharged with nerve energy. The reservoirs of vitality are refilled while I rest in the peace of God."

QUESTIONS FOR DISCUSSION

1. Is it ever the prerogative of "a person of faith" to "dictate" to God the method by which a healing is to take place?

2. Can tiredness ever be considered a sin?

3. Should we expect to be healed from organic and structural illness as well as from psychosomatic sickness?

4. Is the healing process dependent upon a person's cooperation? If so, how can a person seeking healing discover what is his/her responsibility in the healing process?

Lesson No. 8: Hindrances to Healing

The most frequent question asked in relation to healing is this: "why wasn't I healed when I prayed for healing?" or "why wasn't 'so-and-so' healed as a result of an active intercessory prayer ministry on his/her behalf?" Such questions compel us to face realistically this issue and to seek to discover those factors that can be hindrances to healing.

At the outset we must keep in mind certain basic assumptions: (1) God does not act arbitrarily in the granting of healing power; (2) healing is not dependent upon a person's relationship to a human "healer"; (3) healing is in accordance with spiritual laws. (See Lesson No. 6 "The Healing Steps.")

At least two predominant myths have developed in relation to the failure to be healed: (1) that such failure is the sure evidence of a lack of faith on the part of the one seeking healing; (2) that such failure is related to the will of God who does not purpose that a certain person be healed. We must disabuse our minds at once of these myths and the assumptions upon which they are based.

The absence of the right kind of faith, anticipatory faith, can be a major hindrance of healing, as we shall see later in this discussion. But the lack of faith cannot be considered the sole measurement to be applied in every case of failure.

I think at once of several individuals on behalf of whom I have participated in active healing ministries - a missionary, a house wife, a building contractor, a teacher, a minister. These individuals were not healed in this life-the healing of eternity is reserved for them. But every evidence points in the direction that the failure to be healed was in no sense the result of any lack of faith on their part. Each of them was a person of radiant, confident, persevering, hopeful faith.

The second myth is also prominent. This is the idea that whenever a person is not healed it must be God's will that he/she not be healed. At once this assumption is seen to be diametrically opposite to the conviction that God wills wholeness for every person. (See Lesson No. 4 "A Theology of Healing.")

What, then, are some of the factors which may be identified as hindrances to healing? Many authors have written on the subject. One of the most illuminating discussions of this entire area is to be found in Chapter 3 in *God's Healing Power* by the late Edgar L. Sanford. In the list that follows, ten of the hindrances were suggested in this particular chapter. I have provided the discussion for each of these and also added another hindrance - the absence of compassion (No. 5).

1. The Negativism of the Secular World

The climate of the secular world in which we are compelled to live is one of distrust in the supernatural and doubt concerning miraculous happenings in human experience. A sinful and faithless world exudes unhealthy spiritual air which even faithful souls must breathe. The seeker after healing must elevate his soul continually into the pure air of spirituality.

2. The Negativism of the Christian World

An even greater tragedy is the fact of negativism within the Church itself. In far too many instances the contemporary church lives in a vague atmosphere of uncertain belief and dubious allegiance. Too often the individual sincerely seeking healing finds himself more or less alone, even in the midst of professing Christians.

3. The Negative Influence of Others

One of the greatest obstacles to faith for healing is the negative influences of friends and neighbors, sometimes even members of one's own family. It is difficult for a person to become confident of God's healing power when he or she hears continually words of disbelief in relation to divine healing. One who would receive God's healing power must learn to live above this negative influence. One's entire confidence must be in God continually.

4. The Absence of Spiritual Motivation

Spiritual motivation includes a number of areas: (1) the end for which the healing is to be used, the deepest reason for the seeking of the healing; (2) one's own spiritual purging as a prerogative for the seeking of healing in other areas of his personality (see Lesson No. 6 - healing step No. 2); (3) the full use of spiritual methods in the seeking of healing.

5. The Absence of Compassion

The healing miracles of Jesus were motivated by His compassion for people. Jesus earnestly desired that all people should experience wholeness. Healing power cannot flow where compassion is lacking. Both the person seeking healing and all those who participate in the healing ministry must be channels of God's redeeming and healing love.

6. Old Age

The matter of aging years can present a real conflict in one's thinking about healing. Humanly speaking, it is easier to renovate a human body that is resilient with youth than a body that is wearing out with age. But, spiritually speaking, it is often more natural for a mature person of older years to manifest faith in the direction of personal healing.

7. Environmental Confusion

Sometimes the very atmosphere of one's environment reacts unfavorably upon one's receptivity to spiritual blessings. If one's circumstances are characterized by restlessness, anxiety, fearfulness and the like, it becomes increasingly difficult for the individual to escape personal distraction and tension. Such confusion impedes the flow of God's healing power.

8. Discouragement

No matter what its cause, the mood of discouragement is always a hindrance to healing by any means. Every effort must be made to remove the cause of discouragement. The patient must face his situation realistically and not become preoccupied with conditions beyond his control. He must free himself from tension created by discouragement. He must discipline himself to trust in God, in relation to all things.

9. The Lack of Anticipatory Faith

Of all the obstacles to healing, this is among the most strategic.

Faith must be seen in its true content. It is not enough to say "I believe in God," or "I believe in a God who is all-powerful," or "I believe in a God who is able to heal." These are necessary basic steps in faith for healing, but they do not go far enough. Faith also says "I believe that God will heal; I believe that God is healing now."

Such faith becomes a present, power-producing, life-changing, personal reality. And as such it is essential for healing.

10. The Continuance of The Factors that Caused the Illness in the First Place

In nearly three quarters of the cases of illness, causes for these functional illnesses are to be found in mental, emotional, and spiritual factors. Until these factors which contributed to the illness in the first place are eliminated, the resulting illness will continue. For illustration, guilt can cause functional disturbances. In such cases, healing becomes impossible until the factor of guilt is resolved in a Christian manner.

In the purely physical areas, we cannot expect healing if we persist in violating the laws of good health. We need often to pray with Richard Wong:

"Forgive us, our Father, for our enthusiasms for the illegal and the impossible things. . .jet speeds on the crowded highways. . .private arithmetic to use on tax forms. . . and hopes that pies and cakes do not add inches. So root us in the facts of life and discipline us to face the awful truths we would hide from. Amen." (*Prayers from an Island*)

11. Certain Unknown Factors

We must admit, that just as there lies before the medical world a vast realm of unexplored knowledge, so in the spiritual realm there are factors influencing success or failure in healing of which we are ignorant. It is our hope that someday, in our progress in the field of healing, even these factors will be made known to us. Until then we must commit even our "ignorance's" to the wisdom of God. After all we are finite creatures, dealing with infinite power.

A closing word is in order. Failures do not invalidate the ministry of healing. If a doctor has treated a patient who dies, he does not give up his practice. A medical doctor, also a psychiatrist, who is a committed Christian, in affirming that failures do not nullify the Church's ministry of healing, said to me in private conversation: "The Church does not stop the work of evangelism because all do not accept Jesus Christ as Savior. Nor should the Church fail to engage in a healing ministry because all are not healed."

The contemporary church as the body of believers is not being true to the New Testament portrait of the church if it seeks to evade its responsibility as a healing community simply because healing does not always result. Rather should the church examine itself in the light of God's word to see if it is in anyway responsible for such lack of healing.

QUESTIONS FOR DISCUSSION

1. Why is it imperative that one have a correct view of the nature of God if he/she is to engage in an effective healing ministry?

2. Can you recognize the presence of any of these hindrances to healing in the experience of people you know who are not healed? In your own case when you were not healed?

3. Are you the kind of person that can be a positive influence upon another person who is seeking healing?

4. How can you help to develop in your local church a climate of faith for healing?

Lesson No. 9: Prayer and Healing

I want to begin this lesson on an extremely personal note. As far as I can remember the first article that I ever wrote on healing was in relation to prayer and healing. It was written in 1946, five years before I began my active healing ministry. It appeared in the daily devotional *The Upper Room*, under the date of August 17th.

Writing on the passage in Acts 9:40-41, I penned the following:

Jesus Christ, the great physician, associated prayer and healing in an indissoluble relationship. He prayed before He healed; He thanked God for the healing which He accomplished. He told His disciples that works of healing came only as the result of prayer and fasting.

Moreover, prayer and healing were maintained in a vital association in the early Christian Church. The first-century Christians were told to resort to prayer, and they were assured that "the prayer of faith shall save the sick, and the Lord shall raise him up."

Just so today, prayers may be utilized as an essential element in all healing. This does not mean to neglect the advantages of modern medicine; rather it emphasizes the power of prayer upon the total personality. Dr. William Sadler, an eminent physician, has declared that in neglecting prayer for healing we are neglecting the greatest single power in the healing of disease.

Many have written concerning the strategic relationship between prayer and healing. It will be both inspiring and reassuring to hear some of these words:

> "A life open to God in faithful prayer is open to agencies of healing beyond the range of medicine and surgery."
>
> > -W.E. Sangster, D.D.

> "Prayer is a means of reaching this healing power of the Lord and giving it a channel to flow through, that body and soul may be helped to work together in harmony, their association unblocked and unbroken."
>
> > -Gwynne Dresser Mack

> ". . . God has bound Himself in certain activities to the prayers of His people, and unless they pray, He will not act. Heaven may will something to happen, but Heaven waits and encourages earth's initiative to desire that will, to will and pray that it happen. . .God has willed that His hand be held back while He seeks for a man, an intercessor to plead 'Thy will be done on earth.'"
>
> > -R. Arthur Mathews

"Prayer is a force as real as terrestrial gravity. As a physician, I have seen men, after all other therapy had failed, lifted out of disease and melancholy by the serene effort of prayer. It is the only power in the world that seems to overcome the so-called 'laws of nature'; the occasions on which prayer has dramatically done this have been termed 'miracles.'"

-Alexis Carrel, M.D.

"Prayer tends to counteract the physiological effects of anxiety, it favors better sleep, and stimulates one to better efforts." (In this statement, Paul Dudley White, M.D. is telling us that prayer can be an effective curative agent.)

"The wise physician 'never discounts the healing power of faith, the handmaiden of prayer. Often he has felt the inward strength and courage of a patient about to undergo a serious operation. He has seen the remarkable convalescence affected favorably by the faith and prayers of the patient, his friends and relatives who visit him, and of his clergyman. All is well with a man who has established this means of grace and source of inspiration and strength, this hand clasp with God in his daily living.'"

-Garfield G. Duncan, M.D.

"Prayer can have a reassuring effect and can be highly supportive of mental health."

-Nolan D.C. Lewis, M.D.

E.S. Jones reminds us that prayer can bring a continuing healing: "If we are identified with Jesus in prayer as cooperation, then His very life comes out in our bodies, quickening them, reconstructing them, making weak tissues and nerves into strong tissues and nerves. . .This is healing by His very presence within His life coming out in our mortal bodies. . .We cultivate His presence, and He in turn permeates us with His health."

Healing Prayer in the Bible and in the Early Church

The holy scriptures always recognize this vital relationship between prayer and healing. Prayers for healing are prominent in the Old Testament. Here are a few illustrations: "Heal her now, O God, I beseech Thee" (Nu. 12:13); "0 Lord, heal me" (Ps. 6:2); "Heal me, O Lord, and I shall be healed" (Jer. 17:14).

One recalls the Old Testament narrative of the people being bitten by fiery serpents in the wilderness (Nu. 21:6-9). We are told that "the people came to Moses and said, 'Pray unto the Lord, that He take away the serpents from us.' And Moses prayed for the people." The prayer was heard, for God provided a brazen serpent, which became a symbolical medium of healing to the people. In another era King Hezekiah prayed to God for healing, and his life span was extended fifteen years (11 K. 20).

The New Testament is replete with prayers for healing. During the ministry of Jesus many prayers for healing were addressed to Him. (See Jn. 4:46-54; Mt. 8:1-13; Mt. 9:2-8.) Likewise, Jesus uttered prayers upon the occasions of His healings. (See Mt. 1 5 : 29-3 1 ; Jn. 1 1 : 41-43.)

When we move from the ministry of Jesus into the life and activity of the early Christian Church we discover this same prominence of prayers for healing. A detailed study of this subject could be made from the Acts of the Apostles. (See Acts 3:5; 4:29, 30; 5:15, 16; 9:11, 12, 17, 18; 9:32-34; 9:40, 41; 28:3-6.)

The ministry of healing and the relationship of prayer to it, as conducted in the early Church, is summarized in these exhortatory words of the Apostle James: "Is any among you afflicted? Let him pray. Is any merry? Let him sing psalms. Is any sick among you? Let him call for the elders of the church; and let them pray over him, anointing him with oil in the name of the Lord: And the prayer of faith shall save the sick, and the Lord shall raise him up; and if he have committed sins, they shall be forgiven him" (Ja. 5:13-15).

During the two centuries after the closing of the New Testament canon, prayers for healing continued to figure prominently in the ministry of the Christian Church. Evelyn Frost, author of the studious volume entitled *Christian Healing*, presents evidence of a valid healing ministry in the church, as documented in the writings of the ante-Nicene fathers, beginning with Clement of Rome (95 A.D.) and continuing to Lactantius (315 A.D.).

Just so, it could be shown conclusively, if space permitted, that in every period of Church History the practice of Christian praying has included prayers for healing. And today, in the active healing movement of the church, prayer is assigned a significant and vital part. In fact, the climax of every healing service is reached in the prayers for healing.

CHARACTERISTICS OF EFFECTIVE HEALING PRAYER

On the basis of what we have noted already, we discover that the healing power of God comes in response to prayer. At the heart of prayer is sincere spiritual desire. A study of healings reveals the presence of sincere spiritual desire in the supplication which sought such healings. Sometimes the prayer for healing came from the sufferer himself. Sometimes it came from others who were deeply concerned. At other times the prayer was uttered by the Great Physician Himself. But always prayer- sincere spiritual Desire and then healing power in response to it.

What, then, are the characteristics of effective healing prayer?

First, prayer for healing must be sincere. It must grow out of a life of prayer. It must arise out of a sense of real need. It must sincerely acknowledge the only valid source of supply, a divine source. There must be a sense of dedication in the use of the results of the healing prayer.

Second, prayer for healing must be specific. A person must be specific, not general, in his request for healing. An individual must visualize exactly his need and his desire. A person must not be vague. Rather, he must tell God exactly what he wants. Being specific in this manner certainly should not be considered presumptuous by a truly dedicated Christian.

Third, prayer for healing must be anticipatory. Such prayers must be characterized by an eager expectancy, the attitude of an active faith. Never must the one who prays think in terms of failure. Always there should be the anticipation of God fulfilling what He has promised.

Finally, prayer for healing must be appropriating. Prayer reaches its climax in the appropriation of God's gifts by faith in the reception of what God has promised. The person who prays for healing appropriates by beginning to act in the strength of the healing power received.

HOW TO PRAY FOR ANOTHER'S HEALING

The Rev. Dr. Laurence H. Blackburn, Chairman of the Board of Directors of the International Order of St. Luke the Physician and author of the well-known healing volume *God Wants You to be Well*, gives extremely helpful suggestions about praying for another's healing:

1. Have a right relationship with the person for whom you are praying.

2. Do not judge the person for whom you are praying.

3. Try to secure the cooperation of the person for whom you are praying.

4. Pray with hope and expectation.

5. Pray for God's blessing as God may see the need.

6. Continue to pray for the person even when your prayers are resisted.

7. Pray for the person when he/she is asleep.

8. Never try to coerce or cajole God in your prayers.

9. Pray in perfect trust and with love.

10. Pray in utter honesty.

11. Pray without the fear of death.

12. Decide in advance how you are going to respond to your prayer being answered.

HOW TO FORM A HEALING PRAYER GROUP

Intercessory healing prayer groups are an important part of the ministry of healing in the local church. Even though this matter will be discussed in more detail in a subsequent lesson, this is a good place to at least try to answer this question which is often raised: "How is a healing prayer group formed?"

The immediate answer is undoubtedly a general one: a healing prayer group is formed like any other prayer group is formed. The main difference between prayer groups is not in the manner of their formation but in the focus of their spiritual activity. A healing prayer group is focused on learning to pray for healing and then praying for healing.

The late Dr. W. E. Sangster of England, was a leader in the Prayer Group Movement. Listen to what he wrote in his book, *Teach Me To Pray*, concerning how to form an intercessory prayer group:

"Raise with God the question whether you should join some prayer group already in existence or start one. If you are led to start one inquire of God to what one person you should mention the matter first. Pray further about the conversation; seek a suitable time and have an unhurried talk with that person. Tell him or her how God has led you, why you think united prayer so important, and what you hope may come of this venture.

"If, after reflection, the other person agrees to join with you, you have a prayer cell. Two are enough: 'Where two or three are gathered together in my name. . .' Ten or twelve might be regarded as maximum."

QUESTIONS FOR DISCUSSION

1. What is the true nature of prayer?

2. Study the prayers related to the healing miracles of Jesus and note how they fulfill the requirements for healing prayer discussed in this lesson, i.e. (1) sincerity, (2) specificity, (3) anticipatory faith, (4) appropriation.

3. In the light of the New Testament teachings, what is the relation between prayer and fasting?

4. Is God "inspiring" you to be a part of a healing prayer group in your local church?

Lesson No. 10: What Should the Church be Doing?

There are various attitudes concerning the church's relationship to a ministry of healing. There are those who believe that the church should not concern itself with any ministry of healing per se. Such an idea claims support from both philosophical and theological considerations. There is the materialist claim that man's body can be cared for by scientific means alone and thus religious help is superfluous. There are the claims of a Bultmannian theology that there is no supernatural agency which can break through natural law. Some religionists believe that sickness is God's direct and disciplinary gift to men. Others are dispensationalists and teach that the divine gift of healing was authentic only in that particular period when the Christian Church was getting started and that it has been withdrawn in subsequent dispensations.

The other extreme in attitude is found in those who declare that the church is the one true healing agency ordained of God and that it should take the place of all other healing agencies. These folks say, "Let the church do it all. Let the preacher become the 'doctor' and 'surgeon.' Let the worship service, the pastoral counseling session become the 'dispensary,' the 'clinic.' Let there be no reliance on medical science in any of its branches. Meditation and prayers are the only true medicine."

I reject both of the above attitudes as un-scriptural and unrealistic. It seems that in between these extreme attitudes there is to be discovered the authenticity of a valid ministry of healing for the church to participate in. The church never ceases to be under the divine mandate: "Go teach - go preach - go heal."

In this lesson today, on the subject "What Should the Church Be Doing?" I want to present three convictions, in the nature of conclusions, and offer as much documentary evidence as editorial space will permit.

I. Healing is an authentic ministry of the Church.

I say this for at least six reasons:

1. Jesus Christ as the founder of the church inaugurated a ministry of healing. A study of the gospel records reveals that Jesus devoted much of His ministry to healing. Most of His miracles were miracles of healing. In the gospels, there are records of at least 26 healing miracles which Jesus performed on individuals. There are five other references to His healing ministry in respect to "a great multitude," "many people," and "others."

2. The Great Commission which Jesus Christ gave to the church includes the ministry of healing. William Barclay, eminent New Testament scholar, writes: "preaching, teaching, healing - that was the three-fold pattern of the ministry of Jesus. Healing was an inseparable part of His work and of the pattern of the work of His apostles."

3. Healing was a regular ministry in the early Christian church. A study of the Book of Acts and the succeeding New Testament scriptures reveals the six-fold ministry of the early church.

- The **proclaiming** church – 1 Corinthians 1:23,24 - The good news was announced that God's Son, crucified and resurrected, had inaugurated the new kingdom of truth, grace, and power.

- The **teaching** church – Acts 2:42 - Teachers were developed and trained for ministries in Jerusalem, Judea, Samaria, and the "uttermost parts of the world."

- The **celebrating** church - Romans 15:6- With joyous praise and worship the Christians rejoiced daily that Christ was in their midst and that they were serving Him.

- The **fellowship** church – Acts 2:42 - A grateful people were bound together in a close family relationship of mutual trust and ministry.

- The **serving** church – Acts 2:45 - A concern for the poor and a reckless urge to share soon found expression in the organization of deacons.

- The **healing** church – Acts 5:16 - Sick minds and bodies were cured as the apostles were concerned about the whole person.

4. Healing was one of the gifts of the Spirit to the church (Study 1 Corinthians 12:7-11). Healing was one of the "power gifts," to be used "for the common good." I have

a deepening conviction that our concern today ought not to be primarily with whether certain individuals have the gift of healing, but rather with the scriptural concept that healing is a gift for the church to exercise in its redemptive ministry.

5. The church has continued to exercise a ministry of healing through the centuries. Even though such a ministry was not as prominent during the Middle Ages as it was in the first three centuries, yet it continued, and no Christian century has been devoid of an authentic healing witness. The theological rediscoveries of the Protestant Reformation, while not focusing on a healing ministry as such, provided support for such a subsequent ministry of divine grace to the whole person.

6. There is an almost phenomenal resurgence of interest and participation in the healing ministry of the church in the contemporary age. In a very real sense the church is seeking to rediscover its full-orbed ministry.

II. In spite of its resurgence, healing remains largely a neglected ministry in the contemporary church.

I often ask "Why isn't the church more interested in a ministry of healing?" I certainly do not have all the answers. But perhaps there are some insights that will help us understand better the reasons for such a neglect of a healing ministry on the part of the local church. Let me suggest four reasons: (1) Ignorance (2) Unbelief (3) Preoccupation (4) The high cost of a healing ministry.

Ignorance: A host of ministers and laymen are ignorant of the validity of a healing ministry in the local church. Most ministers are the product of their training.

Unfortunately, theological training today does not include emphasis upon the full ministry of healing in the local church.

The knowledge of most laymen about the valid ministries of the church has come from their ministers. If ministers do not teach and explain and utilize the healing ministry of the church, certainly laymen are not to be blamed for their ignorance.

Unbelief: A person or an institution does not carry on an activity unless it is convinced of its validity. As we have noted already, many folks do not believe that the church should engage in a continuing ministry of healing.

Why is this so? For one reason, a lack of knowledge has contributed to an attitude of unbelief. Belief is under-girded by truth. Many have not investigated the historical facts, revealed both in the scriptures and in post-canonical history. A healing ministry has always been a part of the vital spiritual ministries of the church through the ages. If one hasn't been convinced of this, then of course faith is lacking.

For another thing, in this age of vast technological advances, it is easy to maintain a supposed dichotomy between "the spiritual" and "the material." How easy it is to say that it is the church's business to preach the gospel while it is given to medical science to heal the sick.

Also we must face the fact that there are times when people stifle their belief by refusing to act. They have the evidence. They know what is the truth. But they will not act upon it, for many reasons.

Preoccupation: There are those who are so preoccupied with other areas of ministry in the local church, and most of these areas are highly legitimate, that they have never become sensitive to the need of seeking to discover if any valid areas of ministry are still being neglected. There are others who believe in a healing ministry but who do not know how to fit anything else into their already overloaded pastoral schedules and church programs.

The high cost of a healing ministry: It costs something to have a healing ministry. There are the high costs of overcoming the fear of failure, of daring to "go out on a limb for Christ," of developing an ever-deepening Christian compassion, of submitting to the demanding personal spiritual disciplines, of accepting any stigmas that may result, of depending totally upon the Holy Spirit.

III. Healing should become a regular ministry in the local church.

How can this be realized? What steps will make this possible?

Space does not permit a full, even adequate discussion of this vital area. But perhaps I can give some helpful general suggestions about making healing a vital ministry in the local church.

1. We must rediscover the concept of the church as a healing community. The periods in church history when the church has been the most vital have been those when the church ministered most faithfully to the wholeness of persons and of society.

The healing ministry is the responsibility of the total Christian community. "The healing role is given to the congregation, the people of God, who must exercise this dimension of their calling to their sick world in which they live. . . . Man and his society cry out for healing and for wholeness, and where else will they find them but in the therapeutic community which is or should be the church? The church is 'a community of healing' in relation to the total concept of 'salvation and health.' (*International Review of Missions*, April 1968)

2. We must understand the contributions of a healing ministry to the life of the church. Some years ago a study report from the United Church of Christ listed the following contributions which the modern healing movement has made to the church: (1) concern for the individual; (2) focus upon the nearness of God; (3) something happens as a result of prayer; (4) interested in spiritual resources; (5) participation of the worshiper; (6) the whole person is served; (7) prevention of illness.

Let me offer a summary statement in this area. Wherever there has been a vital healing ministry, the church has experienced spiritual renewal.

3. The local church should take advantage of the various opportunities afforded for a healing ministry. Such opportunities are manifold. Let me mention eight of them:

- Teaching and preaching the gospel of health and of healing.

- Providing worship and fellowship opportunities which are genuinely therapeutic in their effects.

- Maintaining a vital revival and evangelistic program. The deepest of all healing is that of the soul in its relationship to God and to others.

- Utilizing the healing power of the sacraments.

- Cooperation with all other legitimate agencies of healing in the community.

- Sponsoring active prayer groups which exercise an intercessory ministry for the healing of needy persons.

- Conducting regular healing services.

- Providing continuing opportunities for healing counseling.

4. All of us must recognize that every Christian is called by God to be a minister of healing. "Everyone who has experienced the healing power of the Risen Christ and whose heart is set on fire by the Holy Ghost is already in His ministry." (*Report of Joint Commission on the Ministry of Healing of the Protestant Episcopal Church*, 1964) "Every Christian has a healing ministry. . . .each of us, regardless of his calling, has a role in the healing community." (Dean Brooks)

In a real sense the ministry of healing is a part of the universal priesthood of all believers.

QUESTIONS FOR DISCUSSION

1. In the light of the practice of the early church, why do you think that healing ceased to be a prominent ministry in the church?

2. What are the evidences of the renewal of the healing ministry in the church today?

3. How can you help a church member who (1) doesn't believe in the healing ministry, or (2) who is prejudiced against the healing ministry, or (3) who doesn't have time for the healing ministry?

4. How can you as an individual be a minister of healing each day?

Lesson No. 11: How To Begin A Ministry Of Healing In A Local Church

Throughout this series of lessons we have commented upon the fact that the contemporary church is experiencing a genuine revival of the healing ministry. Some years ago Cyril Richardson spoke prophetically in this regard:

> There can be no question that primitive Christianity was among other things a healing cult. . . . We see today a revival of this concern of the primitive church for the healing of the sick. . . . This movement is to be welcomed in recalling us to forgotten truths and some neglected power of the church. The gospel is not something for the soul alone. It is a message and a power for man's total being body and soul alike.

In the last lesson we noted the ways in which the local church can be participating in a ministry of healing. Among the several things we discussed are the church's opportunity and responsibility to sponsor active intercessory prayer groups and to conduct regular healing services. In response to these suggestions the question is asked regularly as to how to begin a ministry of healing in a local church.

This lesson is an attempt to deal with this subject. As we proceed it will be evident that the material is aimed primarily at the minister, assuming that he will take the lead. However, it will be impossible for any pastor to do this effectively without the full cooperation of dedicated and concerned lay folk.

Therefore, it is hoped that the material in this lesson will be helpful to lay persons who want to assist in inaugurating a ministry of healing in their local churches. Whatever your position, study this lesson and discover the ways in which you can be a participator in such an undertaking.

Let me offer my suggestions for beginning a ministry of healing in a local church under five general headings.

I. CONVICTION

The pastor and cooperating lay persons must be convinced of the validity of a ministry of healing in a local church. There are various areas of study that will aid in the growth of such a conviction: (1) an understanding of the meaning of healing (see Lesson No. 2); (2) a recognition of the Biblical basis for a healing ministry (see Lesson No. 3); (3) an adequate theology of healing (see Lessons No. 4 and 5); (4) the facing of the fact that most contemporary persons desperately need some kind of healing and that a loving, redeeming God has made provision for such healing (see Lesson No. 1).

II. COMMUNICATION

The pastor who is becoming increasingly convinced of the validity of a healing ministry and who desires to inaugurate such a healing ministry must participate in effective communication with his people concerning the important truths in this spiritual realm which are emerging in his mind and heart.

There are several "natural" ways in which the pastor can communicate effectively with his people concerning his growing convictions in the area of healing. He can speak of them in appropriate counseling sessions and pastoral visitations to the sick. He can let illustrations in his sermons, from time or time, bear testimony to the reality of healing. In his midweek Bible studies, he can occasionally give a series which includes the miracles of Jesus. And when he discusses the healing miracles, he should emphasize their literal healing aspects as well as their spiritual lessons. How prone we are, in speaking of the miracles, to talk in a vein like this: "The miracle of Jesus healing a blind man means that Jesus is able to open the blind eyes of a man's soul"; or "The miracle of healing the impotent man at the pool means that Jesus is able to make a man spiritually sound." Should there not be occasions when we are content to say that Jesus healing a blind man means that He is able to give sight to blind eyes and that Jesus healing an impotent man means that he is able to restore wholeness to a person's body?

The pastor will reach a climax in his communication with his people when he presents a series of sermons on the subject from his pulpit. These sermons should be the homiletical embodiment of his convictions. The truth concerning healing should be presented clearly and persuasively. And it would be helpful if a period of questions and discussion could be held between the sermons in the series.

Just so, the concerned lay person can participate effectively in this entire process of communication. As the lay person continues his/her studies and becomes increasingly convinced, there are innumerable ways for sharing such convictions with others - in private conversations, in sharing in prayer and bible study groups, in personal witnessing, in Sunday school class discussions, and in periods of family devotions. Certainly a Sunday school teacher has an excellent opportunity to communicate convictions through the prepared lessons and in personal contacts with members of the class.

III. COMMENCEMENT

There will come an opportune time for the beginning of a healing ministry in the local church. Perhaps the earliest form of this will be expressed in the formation of prayer groups, whose chief purpose will be that of intercessory prayer for healing. Or perhaps the healing ministry will commence with the holding of regular healing services.

Let me share my own experience in relation to healing services. There is a divergence of opinion about whether such services should be public. I am convinced that they should be. For many years, in my local church, I held such a public healing service once a month.

Even though the healing service would be open to the public, I think that only those individuals seriously interested in the relation between religion and healing should be urged to be in attendance. The healing service should be conducted in a place that is suitable for meditation and devotion, and during such a service ample opportunity should be given for such personal meditation.

A healing service can be conducted in the following sequence:

- Period of private meditation and prayer: focusing of attention upon the healing Christ.

- Scripture: the reading of one of the healing miracles of Jesus Christ.

- Prayer, by the leader.

- Testimonies to healing, by those present.

- Brief message: by the leader, on some phase of the healing ministry. The field is unlimited - scripture incidents, the laws of health, the principles of healing, contemporary testimonies to healing, questions that have been asked about healing, etc.

- Prayers for the healing of those present and the laying-on-of-hands.

- Period of intercession for healing of those not present.

- Benediction.

For the period of prayer for the healing of those present, those interested in receiving such healing for themselves should be invited to come forward, with bared head, and kneel at an altar rail. Then together the supplicants could use such a prayer as this:

Lord, I know that Thou canst heal me. Fill me at this moment with Thyself. Let every part of me - body, mind, spirit – be filled with new life, for Thou art life. Cleanse and forgive me of all sin and make me whole. Heal me so that I may be an instrument of love in Thy service. Amen.

Then could follow the laying on of hands by the minister, accompanied by a brief prayer for healing for each person individually.

After the service of the laying on of hands, it is usually in order to have a period of intercession, during which those in attendance would be asked to intercede personally and collectively for those persons not present who are known to be in need of definite healing and for whom prayer is requested.

IV. COUNSELING

A ministry of healing in a local church must be undergirded by enlightened and sustained counseling. People must be helped to understand the difference between imagined and real sickness. (Unfortunately, imagined sicknesses can become real sicknesses if not dealt with in time.) People who are really sick must be aided in understanding the true nature of their sicknesses and in diagnosing the causes. People must be directed to the most effective healing agency. The work of the minister in a healing ministry requires dedicated skill in the matter of referrals to others.

In those cases where people will be seeking definite healing through the church's ministry of healing, they must be prepared for the laying on of hands at a healing service by being instructed concerning the six healing steps. (See Lesson No. 6).

From time to time there must also be careful counseling concerning the barriers to healing. (See Lesson No. 8).

Because of the importance of counseling in an effective healing ministry it would seem logical to conclude that the Church's ministry of healing finds its most appropriate setting as an integral part of the regular spiritual ministry of the local church.

V. CONTINUITY

Once a healing ministry is inaugurated in a local church, it should be carried on with dedicated regularly. I believe that such a healing ministry should remain at all times under the spiritual leadership of the pastor. This does not minimize the spiritual significance of lay persons in such a healing ministry. It only guarantees a continuity in leadership that will result in growth and enlarged spiritual effectiveness.

Jesus Christ has commissioned His church to a ministry of healing. His words "Go preach, teach, heal" have timeless relevance. And whenever the church engages in a ministry of healing in accordance with the objective and principles of such a ministry as outlined in the New Testament, spiritual renewal always results.

QUESTIONS FOR DISCUSSION

1. How would you respond if your minister asked you to help him inaugurate a ministry of healing in your local church?

2. Should a lay person suggest to a minister that he should begin a healing ministry in the church?

3. How many interested people does it take for a local church to begin a healing ministry?

4. How can the minister and the lay person cooperate fully in the continuance of a healing ministry in the local church?

Lesson No. 12: A Concluding Study

We have now completed eleven studies in The School of Healing. Let us review the areas that we have covered. We have noted the universal interest in healing across the centuries, and the particular concern for healing in our age (Lesson No. 1). A satisfying definition of healing was presented, analyzed and applied (Lesson No. 2). A third lesson sought to establish, at least in general terms, a biblical basis for healing. Two lessons (No. 4 & 5) focused on five basic tenets in an adequate theology of healing. The healing steps and a detailed procedure for seeking healing were then considered (Lessons No. 6 & 7). The extremely practical area of hindrances to healing was dealt with in Lesson No. 8. A lesson was devoted to a consideration of prayer and healing (No. 9). The last two lessons (Ns. 10& ll)were concerned with an active ministry of healing in a local church: the nature and extent of such a healing ministry and how to inaugurate it.

In this closing lesson, I would like to attempt several things: (1) a summary of my basic convictions in the area of healing; (2) a noting of some misconceptions about healing that need to be avoided; (3) the presentation of some predictive ideas about the healing ministry in the future ; and

(4) a listing of some basic books in the field of healing for the person who wants to make further serious studies.

SOME BASIC CONVICTIONS

• Healing is one of the ministries which Jesus Christ has committed to His church. When the church fails to engage in such a healing ministry it is not being fully obedient to its Lord. Participation in such a ministry of healing is one of the requisites for the spiritual renewal of the church in our day.

• God wills wholeness for the total person. It is a pagan rather than a Christian concept to assume that God hands out suffering and permits evil because they are essential ingredients in the formation of spiritual character and the fulfillment of spiritual ministry. Jesus Christ did not divide a person into body and soul, but He saw him as a whole person. He came to save persons, not just souls. Sickness of the mind and body was part of that kingdom of Satan Christ came to destroy!

• There is no solitary and exclusive method of healing. There should be no divisive tension between so-called "material" and "spiritual" methods of healing. The healing ministry of the church employs every healing method. All healing, by whatever method it is accomplished, is of God.

• Healing is not achieved through any magical means or haphazard methods, through any hocus-pocus or sleight of hand. The laws of healing have been revealed and the healing steps are relevant for every person seeking healing. In the final analysis God's healing power flows in response to "authentic prayer."

- Every Christian is called to be a minister of healing. Every person who has experienced the power of the risen Christ, who is "in Christ," whose regenerated heart is set on fire by the Holy Spirit, is always in the healing ministry.

- There are no ultimate failures in the Church's ministry of healing. The highest healing is always a person's right relationship to the living Christ.

MISCONCEPTIONS ABOUT HEALING

We must beware of and avoid being influenced by any of the following misconceptions about healing:

- That the only sicknesses Jesus healed were psychosomatic.

- That the divine commission to heal has been withdrawn from the church.

- That salvation and wholeness are not necessarily related; that it is possible to save a "soul" without saving a "person."

- That the church has no business talking about "the gospel of health" or "the gospel of healing."

- That the healing ministry is restricted to physical healing.

- That the achievement of healing is the result of magic, hocus-pocus, or sleight of hand.

- That the failure to be healed is always the result of a lack of faith.

- That the gift of healing is indissolubly related to other spiritual gifts, particularly the gift of tongues.

- That the healing ministry is not authentic unless everyone is healed.

- That everything that happens to a person is the will of God.

- That the use of material means and methods of healing is a denial of faith.

- That the exercise of the healing ministry is reserved for a "select few."

- That Satan can effect true healing.

FUTURE TRENDS

Even though I am not a "prophet," I would venture some predictions about the healing ministry of the church in the future.

- The healing ministry of the church will continue to grow and expand rapidly. It will find continually enlarged expressions in spiritually sensitive congregations. It will aid greatly in the recovery of the prophetic and priestly ministries of the church.

- The healing ministry of the church will demand a deepening understanding of the true nature of prayer. Healing is always in response to prayer. True intercession is when a person is so aligned with the purposes of God that he becomes the channel of God's healing power to others.

- There will be increasing explorations into the full extent of the healing power of Jesus Christ. Vast strategic areas beckon us forward.

    - Much progress needs to be made in relation to the healing of the emotions. How can a person really be healed of his self-centeredness? How can hate be turned into love?

    - What about the healing of alcoholics, sexual perverts, homosexuals? What can be done with a new generation who profess to be finding religious ecstasy and satisfaction in drugs and "trips"?

    - The healing power of Christ must be explored in relation to every known physical ill. For illustration, the healing of cancer is more than a scientific challenge: it is also an opportunity in the spirit realm.

- There will be a growing cooperation between doctors and "churchmen" (clergy and laity) in relation to healing. Much progress has already been made in this area. The medical profession is becoming increasingly aware of the relation between spiritual faith and healing. There are innumerable illustrations of "healing teams" (doctors and clergymen) at work today.